HOW ELECTRIC AND HYBRID CARS WORK

Nick Hunter

Gareth Stevens
Publishing

Please visit our website, www.garethstevens.com. For a free color catalog of all our high-quality books, call toll free 1-800-542-2595 or fax 1-877-542-2596.

Library of Congress Cataloging-in-Publication Data

Hunter, Nick.
How electric and hybrid cars work / by Nick Hunter.
   p. cm. — (EcoWorks)
Includes index.
ISBN 978-1-4339-9561-3 (pbk.)
ISBN 978-1-4339-9562-0 (6-pack)
ISBN 978-1-4339-9560-6 (library binding)
1. Hybrid electric cars — Juvenile literature. 2. Electric automobiles — Juvenile literature. I. Hunter, Nick. II. Title.
TL220.H86 2014
629.2293—dc23

OCT – 9 2013
KIDS
629.2
HUN

First Edition

Published in 2014 by
Gareth Stevens Publishing
111 East 14th Street, Suite 349
New York, NY 10003

© 2014 Gareth Stevens Publishing

Produced by Calcium, www.calciumcreative.co.uk
Designed by Simon Borrough and Paul Myerscough
Edited by Sarah Eason and Ruth Bennett

Photo credits: Cover: Dreamstime: Gyuszko. Inside: Audi: 24; Dreamstime: Lcro774, Madajimmy 5; Shutterstock: 8, Artens 2, 11, Darren Brode 16, Hung Chung Chih 21, Patrick Foto 28, James A. Harris 22, Johnbraid 6, Zoran Karapancev 26, Kavram 17, Yuriy Kulik 9, LovelaceMedia 18, Miker 10, Susan Montgomery 12, Mypokcik 15, Nikonaft 7b, Federico Rostagno 23, Fedor Selivanov 14, SF photo 27, Michel Stevelmans 25, SVLuma 7t, Thampapon 19, Maksim Toome 29, Topora 20, Faiz Zaki 1, 13.

Printed in the United States of America

CPSIA compliance information: Batch #CS13GS: For further information contact Gareth Stevens, New York, New York at 1-800-542-2595.

OCT – 2 2013

Contents

Cars Clean Up

Have you heard of an electric or hybrid car? These cars are in the news all the time—you might have read about celebrities driving hybrid cars or seen pictures of them in magazines. So, what is so special about these cars and how do they work?

Take a Look Inside

Conventional cars have an internal combustion engine, which runs on gasoline. Electric cars are different—under the hood is an electric motor, which runs on electricity. The car is powered by batteries, which are recharged by plugging the car into an electric socket, just like recharging your cell phone. A hybrid car uses two energy sources to power it—the most common hybrid cars have a gasoline-powered engine and an electric motor.

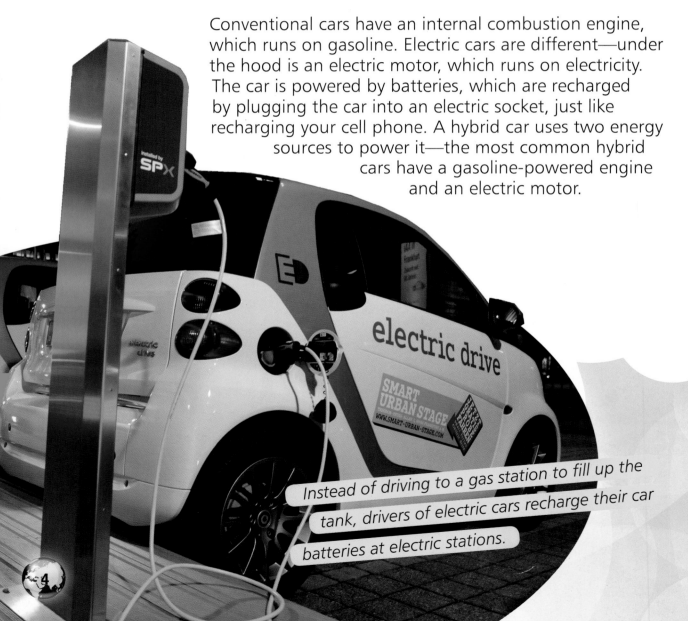

Instead of driving to a gas station to fill up the tank, drivers of electric cars recharge their car batteries at electric stations.

Hybrids Up Close

The first electric car began life as a gasoline-powered Geo Prizm. Here are the modifications that took place to turn it into an all-new, clean machine:

- Gasoline engine removed.
- Clutch assembly removed, but transmission left in place.
- New electric motor attached to the transmission.
- Electric controller added to the new electric motor.
- Battery tray installed in the floor of the car.
- Batteries placed in the tray.
- Charger added so that the batteries could be recharged.

The Future Is Green

Hybrid cars are just the start of a new wave of vehicles we are likely to see on our highways. These cars might be making the news today, but if the future really is green, they will be the regular cars of tomorrow.

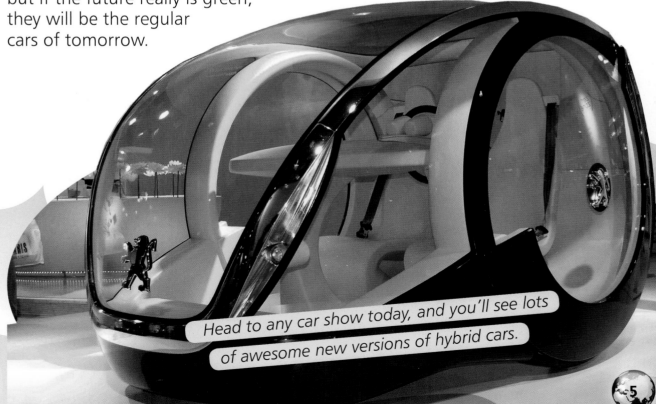

Head to any car show today, and you'll see lots of awesome new versions of hybrid cars.

How Cars Work

Today there are nearly 1 billion cars on the road and most are powered by gasoline engines. This has not always been the case. When they were first developed, internal combustion engines were noisy and unreliable. However, the engines were improved and soon they were used in almost all cars.

Burning Fuel

Internal combustion engines get their name because fuel is burned (combusts) inside a sealed cylinder to drive the engine. An internal combustion engine is fueled by gasoline, which is extracted from crude oil. Gasoline, or gas, releases lots of energy when burned.

The Ford Model T, launched in 1908, was the most successful car of the early 1900s. It was powered by an internal combustion engine.

6

The Perfect Fuel?

Engines fueled by gasoline allow cars to move at high speeds and travel long distances. The fuel can be carried around in the car's fuel tank, and the cars are easy to refuel. However, gasoline also has some serious disadvantages. The developers of hybrid cars are hoping that they can provide a better alternative.

Modern cars include large SUVs with powerful engines, which can travel only a few miles for each gallon of gas they use.

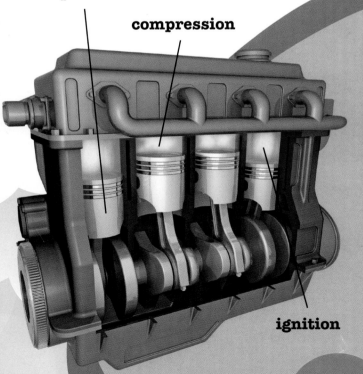

piston

compression

ignition

Internal Combustion Up Close

In an internal combustion engine, hundreds of tiny explosions take place every minute to drive pistons and rotate the car's wheels. This is usually a four-stage process:

- Intake: Mix of gasoline and air is taken into the cylinder.
- Compression: Piston rises up through the cylinder to compress the fuel and create a more powerful explosion.
- Ignition: Spark from a spark plug ignites the fuel, pushing the cylinder downward.
- Exhaust: Fumes created by the fuel are released from the cylinder and the process begins again.

Car Trouble

The invention of the internal combustion engine has changed the world. Cars give people freedom to travel, and it is hard to imagine our societies without them. However, conventional gasoline-powered cars are the source of many problems in the modern world.

Trucks are powered by diesel engines. Diesel also comes from oil and causes air pollution.

The Oil Industry

The process of finding and refining gasoline is one of the world's biggest industries. Gasoline is extracted from crude oil. This oil is formed from the remains of living things that died millions of years ago. Once oil is all used up, it will be impossible to replace.

Searching for Oil

Oil is found deep underground, and the process of drilling for oil often involves damaging some of the world's most delicate habitats. When things go wrong with oil exploration and transportation, oil is spilled. Plants and animals can be killed and their habitats destroyed forever.

Climate Change

Oil pollution is not the only problem caused by gasoline-powered cars. They also have a huge impact on Earth's climate. Harmful fumes that pollute the atmosphere are released when gasoline is burned in a car engine. This changes the delicate balance of gases in Earth's atmosphere and is causing Earth to become warmer. If this continues, this could be disastrous for all life on Earth.

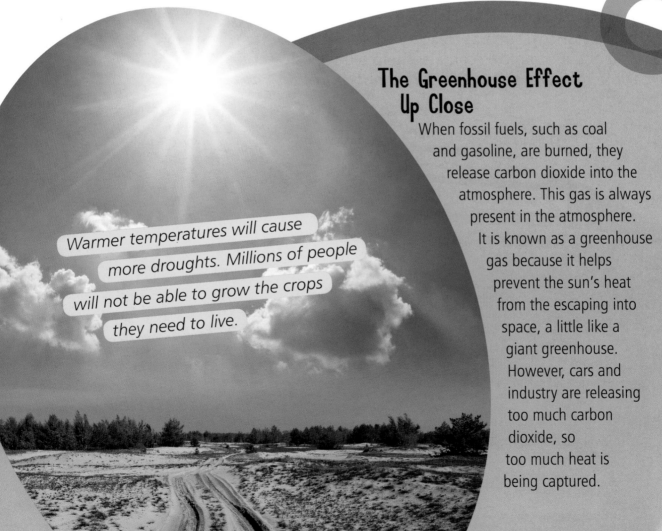

Warmer temperatures will cause more droughts. Millions of people will not be able to grow the crops they need to live.

The Greenhouse Effect Up Close

When fossil fuels, such as coal and gasoline, are burned, they release carbon dioxide into the atmosphere. This gas is always present in the atmosphere. It is known as a greenhouse gas because it helps prevent the sun's heat from the escaping into space, a little like a giant greenhouse. However, cars and industry are releasing too much carbon dioxide, so too much heat is being captured.

The Electric Option

Electric vehicles are now being developed by many different car companies. But, they are still not a practical option for the average car user. What is stopping fully electric cars from appearing on our roads?

Already Here

You may have seen electric vehicles without realizing it. These are usually vehicles that are designed to travel small distances, such as delivery vehicles or forklifts. Small electric vehicles can also help elderly or disabled people to travel around their neighborhoods.

Hybrid buses are used in many cities. They only need to travel at low speeds and hybrid technology makes them quieter as well as reducing carbon emissions.

Early Electrics

Many of the earliest cars were in fact electric. They were quiet and more reliable than early gasoline engines. However, as cars became more popular, internal combustion engines became the only real option for most drivers. Electric cars could travel only short distances before they had to be plugged into an electrical source to recharge their batteries.

In the future, recharging points may be as common as gas stations.

ECO FACT

Electric Drawbacks

Fully electric vehicles are limited because they need to be charged regularly. Of course, refueling conventional cars is made possible only by a network of gas stations. At present, there are few places to charge electric cars, and charging takes much longer than filling a tank with gas.

Types of Hybrid Car

What is a hybrid car? It is any car that is powered by more than one source of energy. Electric motors, solar power, and other technologies all have a part to play in the development of hybrid cars. Most hybrid cars on the road today are powered by a combination of an electric motor and a gasoline engine. They are currently the most realistic alternative to a conventional car because they don't have all of the drawbacks that electric cars do.

Full Hybrid Cars

The most common hybrid car is often called a "full hybrid" car. It is powered by an electric motor alongside a conventional gasoline engine. The electric motor can power the car on its own at low speed, such as when driving in a city. The combustion engine is used at higher speeds.

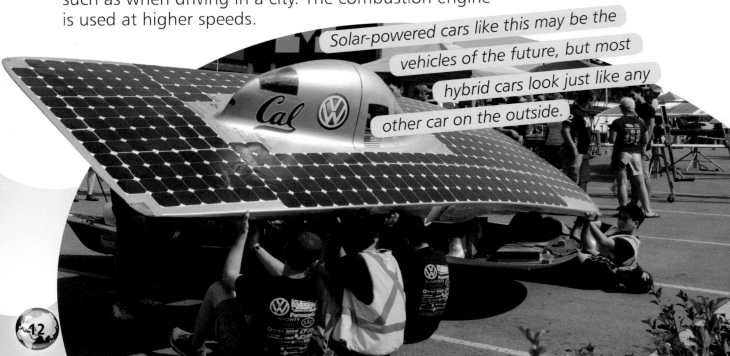

Solar-powered cars like this may be the vehicles of the future, but most hybrid cars look just like any other car on the outside.

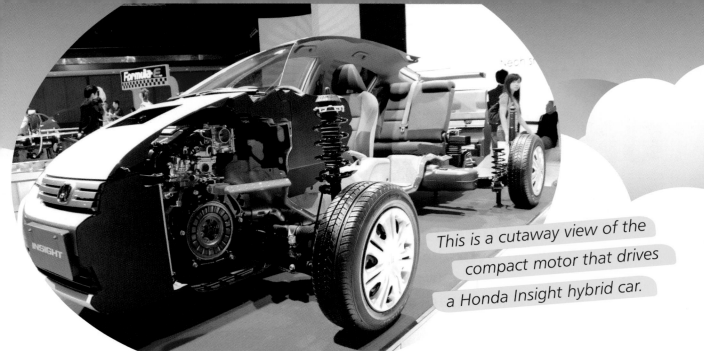

This is a cutaway view of the compact motor that drives a Honda Insight hybrid car.

Mini Hybrids

"Mini-hybrid" cars also have an electric motor, but it only provides extra power—the motor cannot power the car on its own. The electric motor helps to reduce the amount of gasoline that the car uses.

Micro-Hybrids

"Micro-hybrid" cars only make limited use of an electric motor. When the car is stopped at lights or in traffic, the combustion engine shuts off and an electric motor operates. When the car needs to move again, the motor allows it to be ready to start instantly. This saves a small amount of fuel.

ECO FACT

Traveling Light

Although hybrid cars have both internal combustion engines and electric motors, they are much lighter than conventional cars. Hybrid cars have a much smaller engine. This reduces the weight of the car, decreasing the power needed to push it along the road.

13

How Hybrid Cars Work

If you look beneath the hood of a full hybrid car, they do not all look the same. The motor industry is constantly developing new models of hybrid car that are more efficient. Most hybrid car drivetrains fall into two different types: parallel and series hybrids.

The Toyota Prius was one of the first hybrid cars to become popular. This plug-in version can be recharged at home.

Parallel Hybrids

Many of the most common hybrid cars, such as the successful Toyota Prius, operate with their two main power sources turning the same axle. Sometimes the gasoline combustion engine will operate on its own. It may be supported by the electric motor when more power is needed, such as when the car is accelerating. Other parallel hybrids rely mostly on their electric motor, using the combustion engine only for highway driving. The car's combustion engine also charges the battery of the electric motor.

ECO FACT

Computer Control

Computers have a big part to play in how hybrid and electric cars run. They decide when the car should use electric or gas power and they monitor the car's performance.

This Range-Extended Electric Vehicle made headlines when it won a race against 70 other cars. The race was not to finish first but which car would use the least fuel to travel 57 miles (91 km).

Series Hybrids

A series hybrid car includes an electric motor and a gasoline-powered engine, but they are arranged differently from a parallel hybrid. Only the powerful electric motor is actually moving the car's wheels. The gasoline engine is there just to recharge the electric motor. Series hybrid cars are also called Range-Extended Electric Vehicles (REEV) because the engine helps them travel farther but the main motor is fully electric.

Plug-in Hybrids

One of the most recent developments in hybrid technology is the plug-in hybrid. These cars are powered mainly by both a battery and electric motor. Many car companies are developing plug-in hybrid cars. Two of the most well-known models are the Chevrolet Volt and the Nissan Leaf.

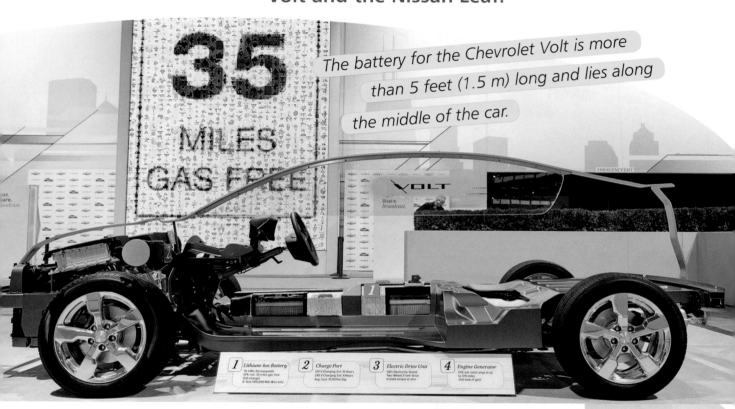

The battery for the Chevrolet Volt is more than 5 feet (1.5 m) long and lies along the middle of the car.

1. Lithium-Ion Battery
2. Charge Port
3. Electric Drive Unit
4. Engine Generator

Plug-in and Go

Plug-in hybrids use their gasoline engine only when their battery charge is below a certain level. This means that for most of the time they are electric cars using no gasoline and with no carbon dioxide emissions. They can be plugged into a home electricity supply, which will charge the battery pack in a few hours.

ECO FACT

Going the Distance

Plug-in hybrids have one major benefit over a fully electric vehicle. A car that has only an electric motor cannot travel far between charges. This is not practical when people expect to be able to drive for hours without stopping. Plug-in hybrids can be used on extended journeys because of their internal combustion engine.

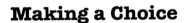

Far from home, or the nearest charging station, power comes from a plug-in hybrid's internal combustion engine.

Making a Choice

Many people expect plug-in hybrids to become more popular than other hybrid cars as technology improves, because they are the cheapest to run and have the lowest impact on the environment. But the plug-in cars available now are not very convenient. When plugged into a electricity supply, the batteries can still take 10 hours to charge fully. When drivers are deciding whether to buy a new car, they think about convenience as well as cost and the environment.

Using Less Fuel

A hybrid car is usually more expensive than a conventional car of a similar size, but they are becoming more and more popular. In Japan, almost 20 percent of new cars are hybrid vehicles. So what is the attraction?

A streamlined car with a low, rounded shape needs less fuel to move it through the air.

Saving Money

As gas prices rise, hybrid cars are becoming popular with drivers who want to reduce their fuel bills. A hybrid car's electric motor dramatically cuts the amount of gasoline it uses. This will save money in the long-term, even though it costs a lot to buy a hybrid car.

Super Efficient

The most efficient electric cars on the road can cover more than 100 miles (160 km) per gallon, using only gas to recharge when away from a power source. Hybrid cars such as the Toyota Prius covered half that distance, but still much more than the average vehicle.

Saving the Environment

Hybrid cars are also bought by drivers who want to reduce the damage that cars do to the environment. Fumes from burning oil products, such as gasoline, pollute the air. The build-up of these waste gases is causing Earth's climate to change. Hybrid vehicles cause less pollution than other vehicles.

Plug-in hybrids such as the Nissan Leaf save money on gas, but their owners will face higher electricity bills when charging the car's battery.

Fuel Up Close

There are several features of hybrid cars that allow them to use less fuel:

- Smaller engines are lighter and need less fuel.
- An electric motor takes over when the car is stopped or traveling at a lower speed, such as in a city.
- When a car brakes, energy is lost, but hybrid cars can recapture this to charge a battery.
- Streamlined designs reduce air resistance.

Reducing Carbon Emissions

In North America, carbon dioxide from transportation makes up around one-third of the typical person's carbon footprint. If a hybrid car uses half as much gasoline as a conventional one, it will also produce half as much air pollution.

Biofuels are made from plants. They can be used in car engines, but there is not enough farmland on Earth to grow the biofuels we would need to replace oil.

Making a Difference

Hybrid cars are a positive step, but we still have a long way to go in the fight against climate change. In 2012, there were around 2 million hybrid vehicles in use in the United States. That sounds like a lot, but it is only a fraction of the 250 million passenger vehicles on American roads.

China is home to four times as many people as the United States. At present, there is only one car for every 20 people in China, but cars are becoming much more popular.

More Change Needed

In many parts of the world, such as in India and China, car ownership is growing fast and most of these cars have conventional engines. Unless hybrid cars become more affordable and more readily produced, climate change as a result of car pollution will continue to be a problem.

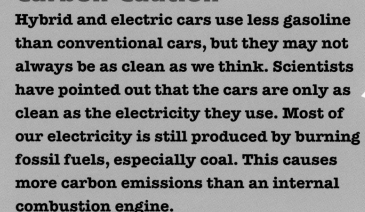

ECO FACT

Carbon Caution

Hybrid and electric cars use less gasoline than conventional cars, but they may not always be as clean as we think. Scientists have pointed out that the cars are only as clean as the electricity they use. Most of our electricity is still produced by burning fossil fuels, especially coal. This causes more carbon emissions than an internal combustion engine.

Hybrid Car Drawbacks

Hybrid cars can match conventional cars for speed and reliability. Cars driven by electric motors are much quieter. Most of all, hybrid and electric cars can save their owners money and help to reduce greenhouse gas emissions. So why doesn't everyone have a hybrid car?

Scientists are warning that the results of climate change, such as melting ice sheets in the Arctic, are much greater than the drawbacks of switching to hybrid and electric cars.

ECO FACT

Too Quiet?

Hybrid cars could also have unexpected drawbacks. One complaint is that hybrid cars are too quiet. Bicyclists or people crossing the street may not hear the cars coming. Some car companies have added extra noise to their cars to prevent this problem.

City streets would be much quieter and less polluted if more people drove hybrid cars.

Still Costly

Hybrid cars are more expensive to buy than traditional cars. The reduced fuel costs act as an incentive to buy a hybrid, but there are other costs involved. All cars need regular servicing and maintenance. The systems that control hybrid cars are often very complex and people worry that the maintenance costs will be high.

Battery Drawbacks

The powerful batteries that drive hybrid and electric cars are being improved all the time but they still have some limits. A typical battery in a hybrid car needs charging every few days. Batteries do not always work as well in cold weather so hybrid car users in cold countries find that they are using the gas engine of their car more often.

High-speed Hybrids

Hybrid cars are known for being clean but not much fun. That's all changing as some of the world's most glamorous car companies are now releasing hybrid cars. High-speed hybrids use the latest hybrid technology to give them extra power and reduce fuel consumption.

The Porsche Hybrid

Porsche is famous for making some of the world's fastest and most exciting cars. Now they are building hybrid cars. The company's 918 Spyder has a top speed of more than 200 miles (321 km) per hour and can accelerate from 0 to 60 miles (0 to 96 km) per hour in fewer than 3 seconds.

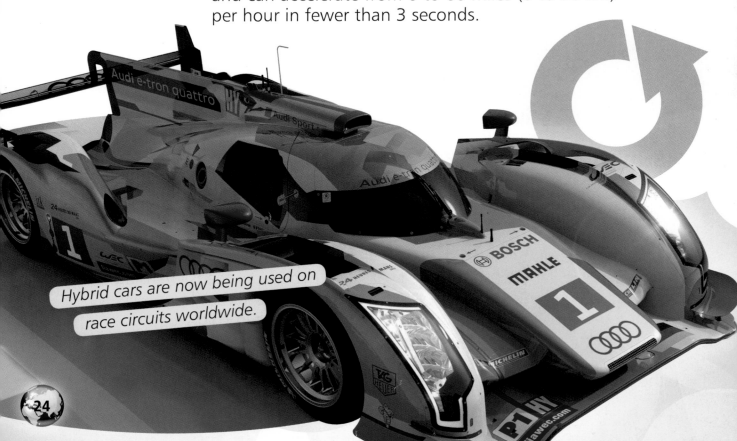

Hybrid cars are now being used on race circuits worldwide.

The Porsche 918 Spyder includes two electric motors alongside its powerful combustion engine. Its makers claim it can cover 78 miles (125 km) for each gallon of gas it uses. Its engine is used less, and so it uses less gasoline.

From Track to Street

Costing close to $1 million, cars like the Porsche 918 Spyder are far too expensive for most drivers. However, technology and design features that are developed for use in supercars often influence the cars that the rest of us drive. These technologies will help to make hybrid cars faster, more efficient, and more attractive to the average car owner.

More and more car owners will be driving hybrid cars in the future.

ECO FACT

Formula 1 Future

Formula 1 race cars now use KERS technology to recover the energy lost when braking and use it for acceleration. There are also plans to modify cars so they run on battery power alone during pit stops.

The Next Step

Scientists are working on many alternative power sources for cars. None of these work as effectively as hybrid cars yet, but a breakthrough could change that.

Presently, hybrid cars are the best solution for cleaner cars, but hydrogen or another power source may provide the key to road travel in the near future.

Power from the Sun

The most powerful energy source available to us is the sun, and many experimental solar cars have been created. There are even races, like the World Solar Challenge, in which solar cars race across Australia. However, storing energy for driving at night is a problem that has still not been solved. Solar cars are also very expensive to make.

Solar Cells

Solar cars are powered by photovoltaic cells in solar panels, which convert energy from the sun into electricity. The cells absorb sunlight and use it to create a flow of particles called electrons. This flow can then be used to charge a battery.

Hydrogen Power

Hydrogen-powered cars may be the solution. They use hydrogen and oxygen to make electricity. The cells continue to produce power as long as they are kept supplied with hydrogen. One day we may all stop to fill up at a hydrogen station.

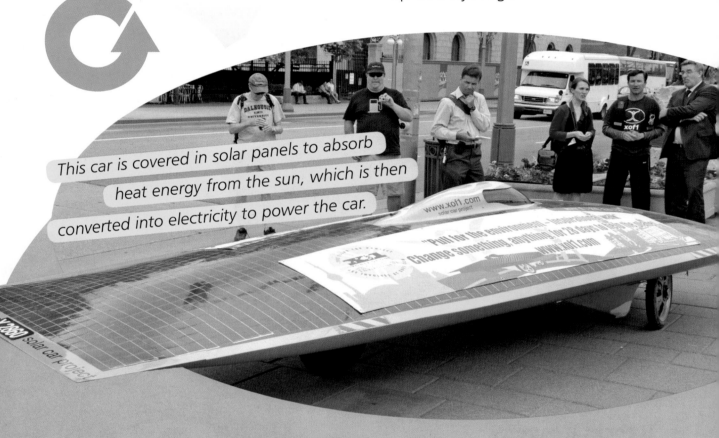

This car is covered in solar panels to absorb heat energy from the sun, which is then converted into electricity to power the car.

Fuel Cells Up Close

Hydrogen fuel cells could power the cars of the future. The fuel cells combine hydrogen and oxygen, which is present in air, to make water. This process generates electricity to power the car. A conventional engine releases carbon dioxide, which harms the environment, but the only waste product of hydrogen fuel cells is water.

Driving into the Future

The future for cars is uncertain. Car ownership is increasing all the time, particularly in countries such as China and India. The number of cars on Earth could grow by 60 percent over the next 20 years. At the same time, scientists are calling for urgent action to tackle climate change.

New fuels cannot offer a solution to road congestion. Public transportation and other alternatives to cars may be the answer.

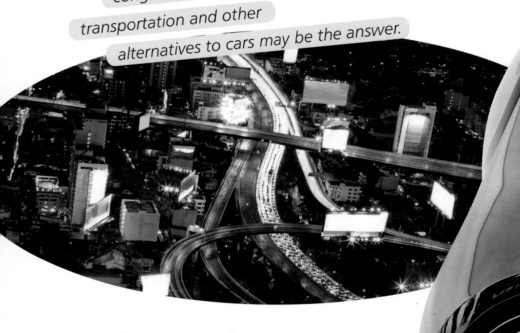

Hybrid Heaven?

A report by a major oil company has predicted that, by 2030, around two-thirds of all new cars will be hybrid, plug-in hybrid, or fully electric. Superlight but tough materials will be developed using new technology so that cars will need less powerful engines.

New materials and design could mean the cars of the future look very different.

Rising gas prices and government attempts to reduce carbon emissions will encourage people to make the switch. But with more and more cars on the world's highways, greenhouse gas emissions will still increase.

Experimental Engines

Experts hope that hydrogen-powered vehicles could lead a transportation revolution. Scientists are also working with other fuels for powering vehicles, such as ultra-cold liquid nitrogen, the substance that makes up most of Earth's atmosphere.

We cannot be certain of the future but it is safe to predict that the cars we drive will be very different.

Glossary

atmosphere the layer of gases surrounding Earth and containing the oxygen that humans and other animals breathe

axle a rod that is fixed to the wheels of a car

carbon dioxide (CO_2) a greenhouse gas that is released when fossil fuels and organic matter are burned

carbon footprint the amount of greenhouse gas emissions caused by a single person or organization

conventional normal or usual, such as conventional cars powered by an internal combustion engine

cylinder a hollow container containing a piston that forms part of an engine

drivetrain all the parts that work together to turn the wheels of a car

electron a small charged particle that is part of tiny atoms from which all matter is made

fossil fuel energy sources formed from the decayed remains of living things, including coal, oil, and natural gas

gasoline a flammable product from crude oil that is used in internal combustion engines

generate to create or produce; for example, electricity

greenhouse gas a gas that absorbs heat in the atmosphere

hydrogen a flammable gas that combines with oxygen to make water

internal combustion engine a type of engine in which motion is created by the burning of fossil fuels with air, as in a car

KERS a way of recovering the energy that a car loses when it brakes. The lost energy is then stored in a battery or another energy-storing device within the car so it can be used later

oxygen a gas that is part of Earth's atmosphere and which humans and other living things breathe

parallel hybrid a hybrid vehicle in which the wheels can be turned by either an internal combustion engine or electric motor

particle a tiny object, such as part of an atom

photovoltaic cell a cell that turns sunlight into electricity

series hybrid a hybrid car in which the wheels are driven by an electric motor alone, supported by a gasoline engine

solar from the sun

For More Information

Books

Callery, Sean. *Victor Wouk: The Father of the Hybrid Car*. New York, NY: Crabtree, 2009.

Goodman, Polly. *Transportation for the Future*. New York, NY: Gareth Stevens, 2011.

Hantula, Richard. *How Do Hybrid Cars Work?* New York, NY: Chelsea House, 2009.

Swanson, Jennifer. *How Hybrid Cars Work*. Mankato, MN: Child's World, 2011.

Websites

Discover more about how electric cars work at:
www.howstuffworks.com/electric-car.htm

This website tells you more about the solar-powered car race across Australia:
www.worldsolarchallenge.org

Take a look at the Smithsonian's collection of experimental vehicles and discover the story of the attempts to develop electric cars:
amhistory.si.edu/onthemove/themes/story_74_1.htmlVisit

Index